Connecting to God

Finding Freedom from Sin

16 Lessons on Romans 1-8

Contents

Introduction

Condemnation The Gospel Saves

Ch. 1 - Condemnation of the Bad

Ch. 2 - Condemnation of the Good

Ch. 3 - Condemnation of the Ugly (Religious)

Introduction

My Story

In High School, I considered myself a great Christian. I went to church, Sunday school, and youth group. I even volunteered to help the poor, lived a moral life, and did well in school. Citizenship awards hung on my wall to prove my value.

When I went to college, my view of Christianity changed when an atheist English professor asked me, "What do you think is the meaning of life?"

I responded, "Life is like a test, if you do well enough you go to heaven."

He raised an eyebrow and exclaimed, "Do you really think the Bible teaches that?"

I went home and began studying the Bible in order to find verses that supported my belief. Over time, I understood that life is not a like a test. God does not save us based on our performance but offers salvation as a free gift.

Realizing that my self worth did not come from awards and leadership positions but from being God's child, changed my life drastically. Since God did not love me based on my achievement, I did not care so much about what others thought about me or my career. Instead of living for my resume, I started studying the Bible, praying, and teaching the gospel to my friends. For the first time, I felt peace.

Though I had learned God's love for me did not depend on my actions, I still struggled with many sins. Pride caused me the most problems. I would look at other people and think I knew better than they. I thought "I don't need to meet weekly with an older believer to help me in my Christian walk and ministry. I can do this on my own." I even started thinking I could run the church better than my pastor!

Knowledge causes pride if not combined with love. In 1 Corinthians 8:1, Paul says, "Knowledge puffs up while love builds up." The constant studying in college caused me to think to highly of myself and not seek out and listen to wise men. I did not know how to use my knowledge to increase my love.

Knowledge does not need to produce pride. Knowledge should produce love as God transforms our mind to think in ways that honor him. Jesus tells us the greatest commandment includes loving God with all of our mind.

I am praying this study will do more than teach you

facts about the Bible and strengthen your debating skills on religious topics. Instead, as you meditate on the gospel, God will transform your mind from thinking about the things of the world to reflecting on the eternal things. The result will be that you stop living for your own desires and comfort, but instead Glorify God by sacrificially serving others.

Our Purpose: To Equip You to Build Christ's Church

Ephesians 4:11-16 (NASB)
And He gave
> *some as apostles,*
> *and some as prophets,*
> *and some as evangelists,*
> *and some as pastors and teachers,*

What did God give?

[12]for the equipping of the saints
> *for the work of service,*
>> *to the building up of the body of Christ;*

Why did God give these gifted people?

What are regular Christians supposed to do?

Luke 6:46-49

2 TImothy
2:15

[13] until we all attain
  to the unity of the faith,
  and of the knowledge of the Son of God,
    to a mature man,
    to the measure of the stature
    which belongs to the fullness of Christ.

What is the goal of our ministry?

[14] As a result, we are no longer to be children,
  tossed here and there by waves
  and carried about by every wind of doctrine,
    by the trickery of men,
    by craftiness in deceitful scheming;

How do we know we are mature?

¹⁵ but speaking the truth in love,
    we are to grow up in all aspects into Him
        who is the head, even Christ,

What do mature people do?

¹⁶ from whom the whole body,
    being fitted and held together
        by what every joint supplies,
        according to the proper working of each
        individual part,
        causes the growth of the body
            for the building up of itself in love.

How do mature people build the Church?

Overview

in this study, we will study how we can connect with God and live in harmony with Him. We will not stop with theoretical head knowledge but push to apply that knowledge to change how we feel toward God and others as well as how we act on a daily basis.

Prayer Requests

Discussion Questions

#1 What training have you had in accurately handling the Word of Truth that has been most helpful?

#2 How confident are you that you could to lead someone to faith in Christ and help them mature in Christ?

#3 What is your strategy to share the gospel with others this semester?

#4 What is your strategy to help other believers grow this semester?

Spiritual Development

Inductively study this passage.

Romans 1:1-7 (ESV)

1 Paul, a servant of Christ Jesus, called to be an apostle, set apart for the gospel of God, 2 which he promised beforehand through his prophets in the holy Scriptures, 3 concerning his Son, who was descended from David according to the flesh 4 and was declared to be the Son of God in power according to the Spirit of holiness by his resurrection from the dead, Jesus Christ our Lord, 5 through whom we have received grace and apostleship to bring about the obedience of faith for the sake of his name among all the nations, 6 including you who are called to belong to Jesus Christ,

7 To all those in Rome who are loved by God and called to be saints:

Grace to you and peace from God our Father and the Lord Jesus Christ.

Observations

Main Point

Interpretation

Applications

Spiritual Development

Inductively study this passage.

Romans 1:8-15 (ESV)

8 First, I thank my God through Jesus Christ for all of you, because your faith is proclaimed in all the world. 9 For God is my witness, whom I serve with my spirit in the gospel of his Son, that without ceasing I mention you 10 always in my prayers, asking that somehow by God's will I may now at last succeed in coming to you. 11 For I long to see you, that I may impart to you some spiritual gift to strengthen you— 12 that is, that we may be mutually encouraged by each other's faith, both yours and mine. 13 I do not want you to be unaware, brothers, that I have often intended to come to you (but thus far have been prevented), in order that I may reap some harvest among you as well as among the rest of the Gentiles. 14 I am under obligation both to Greeks and to barbarians, both to the wise and to the foolish. 15 So I am eager to preach the gospel to you also who are in Rome.

Observations

Main Point

Interpretation

Applications

Prayer

Go Deeper

Pray about when you will spend time with God during the week for personal Bible Study and Prayer.

Pray for a group of friends to meet with for discipleship.

Go Farther

Pray for opportunities to talk with family and friends about Jesus.

Lesson 1

Paul's Introduction :
The Message of the Gospel

History and Location

What is the background of the book of Romans?

Paul had never personally met with the church in Rome.

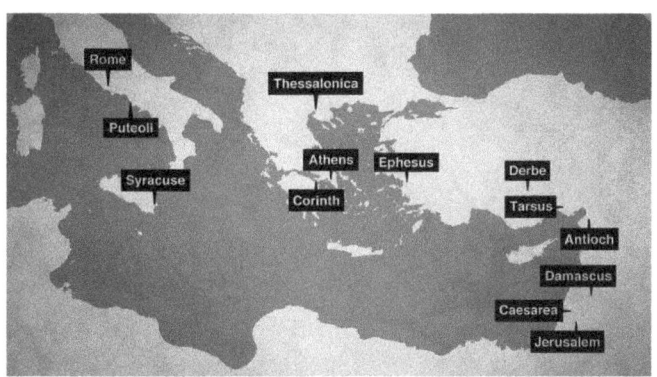

Barry, J. D., Mailhot, J., Bomar, D., Ritzema, E., & Sinclair-Wolcott, C. (Eds.). (2014). DIY Bible Study. Bellingham, WA: Lexham Press.

Romans 1:1-7

a servant by choice

1:1 PAUL, a bond-servant of Christ Jesus, called as an apostle, set apart for the gospel of God, 2 which He promised beforehand through His prophets in the holy Scriptures, 3 concerning His Son, who was born of a descendant of David according to the flesh, 4 who was declared the Son of God with power by the resurrection from the dead, according to the Spirit of holiness, Jesus Christ our Lord, 5 through whom we have received grace and apostleship to bring about the obedience of faith among all the Gentiles, for His name's sake, 6 among whom you also are the called of Jesus Christ; 7 to all who are beloved of God in Rome, called as saints: Grace to you and peace from God our Father and the Lord Jesus Christ.

★ Paul doesn't want to just bring people to Jesus, but he wants them to live it out.

How does Paul view himself?

He sees himself as a bondservant and in a better position than he would be if he was "free."

His introduction echoes the first things he thought about himself.

How do you view yourself?

Paul now offers one of the most full explanations of the gospel found in the Bible.

The Gospel
We know the Gospel is true because:

− Prophecies
− Jesus fulfilled those prophecies

The Gospel focuses on:

Jesus was *the Son of God*

History testifies about Jesus. In fact history is "his-story." God created the earth. Then he created man. Man sinned. God told Adam and Eve that one day, a man born of woman would crush the head of the serpent. This boy would destroy evil and sin.

Since the first sin, people have been waiting for Jesus to fix the problem of sin. Over time, God narrowed down who this boy would be. God told Abraham this man would be one of his descendants. Later He told David he would be one of his descendants. Jesus descended from Adam, Abraham, and David. Jesus fixed the problem of sin by dying on the cross and by raising from the dead. Now we are waiting again for him to come back and to set everything into order.

Jesus is...

Christianity comes from historical fact, not just great philosophy. Jesus predicted his death and resurrection after claiming to be God. Over five hundred people saw Jesus after rising from the dead proving his divinity.

Lord, Liar, or Lunatic
C.S. Lewis taught there are 3 possibilities if someone claims to be God.

1. He is God (Lord)
2. His thinks he is God but is not (Lunatic)
3. He knows he is not God (Liar)

To believe someone's claim to divinity, there needs to be hefty proof. Dying and rising from the dead after predicting you would do so offers the proof needed. Fulfilling prophecies given over thousands of years, makes the case for Jesus divinity even stronger.

Emphasis on Resurrection
Though Jesus dying on the cross is vitally important, almost all the early evangelists emphasized Jesus rising from the dead instead of his death on the cross. Many people died on the cross. Only one person ever rose from the dead after dying on a cross. By rising from the dead, God declared Jesus to be his son.

3. Gave us, grace and apostleship to bring about the obedience of faith

Grace:

Apostleship:

Paul and the other apostles were sent out with authority from God to preach the gospel.

Paul knew his spiritual gift. God gifted him as an apostle.

What is your spiritual gift?

Romans 1:8-10

★ *Paul had never met the Romans, but he was still thankful for them.*

8 First, I thank my God through Jesus Christ for you all, because your faith is being proclaimed throughout the whole world. 9 For God, whom I serve in my spirit in the preaching of the gospel of His Son, is my witness as to how unceasingly I make mention of you, 10 always in my prayers making request, if perhaps now at last by the will of God I may succeed in coming to you.

What did Paul do for the Romans? (1:8-10)

1. He *encouraged* them

2. He *prays* for them

3. He was *thankful for* them

While attending seminary, my college pastor came to speak at chapel. After chapel we had lunch with a number of professors. He told the professors about the ministry I led in college and how God had used it to change many lives. I floated out of the room encouraged. It is important to praise people when they serve God faithfully!

Who should you thank God for because of their example of faithfulness?

Who do you need to encourage because of their faithful service to God?

Who needs your prayers?

Not only did Paul encourage the Romans by letter, he wanted to visit them as well.

Romans 1:11-15

[11] For I long to see you in order that I may impart some spiritual gift to you, that you may be established; [12] that is, that I may be encouraged together with you while among you, each of us by the other's faith, both yours and mine. [13] And I do not want you to be unaware, brethren, that often I have planned to come to you (and have been prevented thus far) in order that I might obtain some fruit among you also, even as among the rest of the Gentiles. [14] I am under obligation both to Greeks and to barbarians, both to the wise and to the foolish. [15] Thus, for my part, I am eager to preach the gospel to you also who are in Rome.

Why did Paul want to visit the Romans? (1:11-15)

1. He was excited to use his spiritual gift to <u>minister</u> to them

2. He was coming ready to <u>receive</u>

3. He was <u>commissioned</u> by God to <u>preach</u> to the whole world.

Paul loved to share the gospel, and he loved to help believers grow to maturity. Paul planned on visiting the Romans to build them up. The Roman church knew Jesus and served Him faithfully, but Paul knew they could benefit from His gift to help them mature as a church. He also looked forward to being encouraged by them as he ministered to them.

When we minister to fellow believers, we go to encourage and serve them, but at the same time, we know that they will encourage us as well. Many of us have experienced this during missions trips. We go to serve but find that we are encouraged and blessed by them as well.

Paul not only looked forward to maturing the church, he also eagerly anticipated preaching the gospel in Rome.

Which area do you struggle with most?

1. Using your gift to help others mature in Christ

2. Allowing others to serve you

3. Sharing the gospel

What do you need to do to grow in that area?

Summary

Paul begins his letter to the Romans by identifying himself with Jesus. He views his life purpose as being set apart for the gospel of God to bring people to obedience of faith.

The gospel tells the good news that Jesus descended from David to his human lineage. God declared him to be His son through the resurrection of the dead.

Paul encourages them for their faithfulness in following Jesus. He tells them of his desire to build them up, to allow them to encourage him, and to preach the gospel in Rome.

Spiritual Development

Memorize Romans 1:16-17.

Read Romans Chapter 1 three times this week on three different days. For accountability, write the date, time and location where you read it each of those three times.

#1

#2

#3

Prayer

Pray for opportunities to encourage growth in other Christians and for opportunities to share your faith.

Discussion Questions

#1 Paul viewed himself as a bond slave and apostle of Jesus sent to share the gospel.

How do you think of yourself? (When you introduce yourself, what do you mention? What is your tag line at the bottom of your e-mail?)

#2 Paul thanked God for the Romans, encouraged them, and prayed for them.

Who should be thanking God for because their faith is well known?

Who do you need to encourage because of their faithful service to God?

Who needs your prayers?

#3 Paul looked forward to going to Rome to serve them, allow them to serve him, and to preach the gospel there.

Which area do you struggle with most?

Serving
Allowing others to serve you
Sharing the gospel

What steps toward growing in that area should you take?

Prayer Requests

Lesson 2

The Gospel Saves

Did your English teacher force you to write a thesis sentence? Mine did. If we did not include a sentence toward the end of our introduction that outlined the rest of the paper, we would not receive an A, even if the rest of the paper was perfect. In fact we might not even get a B. By the end of the year, she would not even grade it. She would just hand it back to us and say, "Fix it."

Paul must have had a greek teacher like my English teacher because he gives us a clear thesis sentence in Romans 1:16-17. As we study the rest of Romans, we will continue to refer back to these verses.

Confidence in the Gospel

In college, our campus ministry would go out and share the gospel with random people on certain weekends. Just the thought of doing that put butterflies in my stomach. I refused to go. My mentor told me he would come by my room and make me go if I did not show up. So I went. Surprisingly people enjoyed talking about what they believe and excitedly discussed their beliefs about God and Jesus.

Three years later, God had changed my heart enough that a group of five or six of us went for a couple hours every Tuesday to share the gospel with groups of students. I saw God use those conversations in my life and in the lives of the other people.

You might be like me and feel uneasy about sharing the good news of salvation that God offers. As we ponder the power of the gospel, it should embolden us to take steps of faith to proclaim its message knowing God will use it to change lives.

In this lesson We will also study the message of the gospel and see that we should feel confident about sharing the gospel.

Romans 1:16-17

[16] For I am not ashamed of the gospel, for it is the power of God for salvation to everyone who believes, to the Jew first and also to the Greek. [17] For in it the righteousness of God is revealed from faith to faith; as it is written, "BUT THE RIGHTEOUS man SHALL LIVE BY FAITH."

How does Paul feel about the gospel message? (1 :16)

What does it mean to be ashamed? (1:16)

"*A painful feeling or feeling of loss of status*"

He experienced loss, but not shame.

What is the gospel?

There are two places in the Bible where Paul lays out the gospel. We saw one last week in Romans 1:1-6. What did Paul tell us about the gospel last week?

REVIEW...

#1 It was prophesied in the scriptures

#2 It is about Jesus

      A. Descendant of David (Fully-Man)

      B. Declared the Son of God by resurrection from the dead (Fully-God)

      C. At Work Now

          1. Gives Grace and Gives Apostleship

          2. Called you to be saints

Another passage that Paul spends a lot of time explaining the gospel is 1 Corinthians 15:1-8.

I Corinthians 15:1-8

15:1 NOW I make known to you, brethren, the gospel which I preached to you, which also you received, in which also you stand, 2 by which also you are saved, if you hold fast the word which I preached to you, unless you believed in vain. 3 For I delivered to you as of first importance what I also received, that Christ died for our sins according to the Scriptures, 4 and that He was buried, and that He was raised on the third day according to the Scriptures, 5 and that He appeared to Cephas, then to the twelve. 6 After that He appeared to more than five hundred brethren at one time, most of whom remain until now, but some have fallen asleep; 7 then He appeared to James, then to all the apostles; 8 and last of all, as it were to one untimely born, He appeared to me also.

Paul summarizes the gospel in two points.

Point 1. (3) *Christ died*

Proof: (4) *Jesus was buried*

Scriptures:

Point 2. (5) *He was raised on the 3rd day*

Proof: (5-7) *He was seen*

Scriptures: *Psalm 16:10*

The gospel includes our response by faith alone.

Galatians 2:14-16

We must accept the Gospel

*But when I saw that their conduct was <u>not in step with
the truth of the gospel</u>, I said to Cephas before them all,
"If you, though a Jew, live like a Gentile and not like a Jew,
how can you force the Gentiles to live like Jews?" [15] We
ourselves are Jews by birth and not Gentile sinners; [16] yet
we know that a person is not justified by works of the law
but through faith in Jesus Christ, so we also have believed
in Christ Jesus, in order to be justified by faith in Christ and
not by works of the law, because by works of the law no
one will be justified.*

How was Peter's conduct not in step with the gospel?

So why is Paul not ashamed of proclaiming the gospel? (1:16-17)

Reason 1: Because it provides salvation.

I Corinthians 1:27

But God has chosen the foolish things of the world to shame the wise, and God has chosen the weak things of the world to shame the things that are strong.

We need to have the attitude of the apostle Paul. We need to confidently hold to the gospel. We need to audaciously share that we can be with God for eternity by grace alone through faith alone in Christ alone.

Reason 2:

Summary

The power of God and the righteousness of God is shown in the gospel. We should confidently share the good news of how Jesus took away our sins and offers us a free gift of righteousness through Jesus death and resurrection. We need to boldly encourage others to receive this gift by faith.

For if we seek salvation, that is, life with God, righteousness must be first sought, by which being reconciled to him, we may, through him being propitious to us, obtain that life which consists only in his favor.
Calvin, Romans Commentary (1:16)

Spiritual Development

Read

Read Romans Chapter 1 three times this week on three different days. For accountability, write the date, time and location where you read it each of those three times.

#1 *Wednesday, September 23 @ 7:15 am in my dorm*

#2 *Friday, September 25 @ 7:30*

#3

Prayer

Pray for opportunities to share your faith this week.

Attempt to have a conversation with at least one person this week as God give you and opportunity.

For accountability record the date, time and summary of the conversation below.

Date/Time:

Summary:

Study

Spend some time doing inductive Bible study on
Romans 1:16-17 and digging it deeper.

Romans 1:16-17

[16] For I am not ashamed of the gospel, for it is the power
of God for salvation to everyone who believes, to the Jew
first and also to the Greek. [17] For in it the righteousness of
God is revealed from faith to faith; as it is written, "BUT THE
RIGHTEOUS man SHALL LIVE BY FAITH."

Observations

Main Point

Interpretation

Applications

Discussion Questions

#1 Many people are nervous about sharing the gospel. What are some reasons that cause you to not share as boldly as the Apostle Paul?

#2 What can you do to overcome the problems in question #1.

#3 Many people claim to be Christians but do not understand the gospel. What are some common areas of confusion that we need to confidently address?

Prayer Requests

Lesson 3

Condemnation of the Bad Person
Romans 1:18-32

This section of scripture addresses some of the biggest questions of our day.

Have you ever thought about what happens to the person who never heard about Christ? How could God condemn him or her?

Have you ever wondered how God responds to people who rejects Him?

How does God view homosexuality? What causes homosexuality?

How does God view people of other religions? Are there multiple ways to God? How does God view people who worship in another religion with more passion and morality than most Christians?

People had similar questions in Paul's day. Paul address them with clarity.

Read 1:18-23

[18] For the wrath of God is revealed from heaven against all ungodliness and unrighteousness of men, who suppress the truth in unrighteousness, [19] because that which is known about God is evident within them; for God made it evident to them. [20] For since the creation of the world His invisible attributes, His eternal power and divine nature, have been clearly seen, being understood through what has been made, so that they are without excuse. [21] For even though they knew God, they did not honor Him as God, or give thanks; but they became futile in their speculations, and their foolish heart was darkened. [22] Professing to be wise, they became fools, [23] and exchanged the glory of the incorruptible God for an image in the form of corruptible man and of birds and four-footed animals and crawling creatures.

What causes the wrath of God to be revealed? (1:18)

Ungodliness + unrighteousness + those who suppress the truth.

↓

("without God")

How can God be fair if he punishes people who do not know better? (1:19-20)

Everyone has "heard" about God because of creation which testifies His existence.

We are without excuse.

"General Revelation"

General Revelation

But you can't just look @ creation and know the Gospel.

No one seeks God unless He's working in their heart. "Special Revelation"

Acquinas Fifth Way

We see that things which lack knowledge, such as natural bodies, act for an end, and this is evident from their acting always, or nearly always, in the same way, so as to obtain the best result. Hence it is plain that they achieve their end, not fortuitously, but designedly. Now whatever lacks knowledge cannot move towards an end, unless it be directed by some being endowed with knowledge and intelligence; as the arrow is directed by the archer. Therefore some intelligent being exists by whom all natural things are directed to their end; and this being we call God (Aquinas, Summa Theologica, Article 3, Question 2).

William Paley - Watch Maker

[S]uppose I found a watch upon the ground, and it should be inquired how the watch happened to be in that place, I should hardly think ... that, for anything I knew, the watch might have always been there. Yet why should not this answer serve for the watch as well as for [a] stone?... For this reason, and for no other; namely, that, if the different parts had been differently shaped from what they are, if a different size from what they are, or placed after any other manner, or in any order than that in which they are placed, either no motion at all would have been carried on in the machine, or none which would have answered the use that is now served by it (Paley 1867, 1).

Special Revelation

How does "the bad person" act? (1:20-23)

1. They profess to be wise.

2. They worshipped man.

3. They worshipped animals.

In this section we see God pouring out his wrath by a three fold progression of giving them over to their sin. God tells man, "If you want to try to find fulfillment in something other than me, go ahead."

Romans 1:24-25

[24] Therefore God gave them over in the lusts of their hearts to impurity, so that their bodies would be dishonored among them. [25] For they exchanged the truth of God for a lie, and worshiped and served the creature rather than the Creator, who is blessed forever. Amen.

God gave them over:

- So the impure lusts of their hearts / all desires of their hearts, not just sexual desires.

Result: Their bodies were dishonored.

Reason: They exchanged truth for a lie

When people quit giving thanks to God, He pours out His wrath on them. God does this passively. He lets them do what they want to. God releases their heart so they no longer worship Him but now worship something else.

Romans 1:26-27

26 For this reason God gave them over to degrading passions; for their women exchanged the natural function for that which is unnatural, 27 and in the same way also the men abandoned the natural function of the woman and burned in their desire toward one another, men with men committing indecent acts and receiving in their own persons the due penalty of their error.

God gave them over:

• Degrading passions

Result:

• Committed indecent acts

After God gives people over to the sexual desires of their hearts, God gives them over to their passions. They no longer sexually desire male to female, but now burn in their sexual passion for people of the same sex.

Romans 1:28-32

[28] And just as they did not see fit to acknowledge God any longer, God gave them over to a depraved mind, to do those things which are not proper, [29] being filled with all unrighteousness, wickedness, greed, evil; full of envy, murder, strife, deceit, malice; they are gossips, [30] slanderers, haters of God, insolent, arrogant, boastful, inventors of evil, disobedient to parents, [31] without understanding, untrustworthy, unloving, unmerciful; [32] and although they know the ordinance of God, that those who practice such things are worthy of death, they not only do the same, but also give hearty approval to those who practice them.

God gave them over:

- A depraved mind
- Improper things

Result:

- Every bad trait manifests itself.
- They get other people to do the same things that they are.

Summary

God pours out his wrath on people by allowing them to do what they want. Since they do not follow God's truth, they start following their own desires and engage in homosexuality. Afterward, they cease to follow God with their mind which results in them engaging in destructive behaviors and encouraging others to do the same.

Discussion

In America, how do you see the progression starting from not giving thanks to God, moving to homosexuality, then to corruption in society?

God's mercy keeps us from falling into these desires.

Where do you see people professing to be wise in today's society?

How do our friends exchange the glory of God for something else?

If you're not growing in your relationship with God, you're declining! You can't really stay put.

What people or things do our friends worship?

Have you ever known someone who knew what they were doing was wrong, but not only did they do it but tried to get others to do it too?

Prayer keeps us less self-absorbed

Spiritual Development

Memorize Romans 1:18

Read

Read Romans Chapter 2 three times this week on three different days. For accountability, write the date, time and location where you read it each of those three times.

#1

#2

#3

Pray

Write the names of at least 1 person you know that fits this category and pray for him/her every day this week.

As a result of your prayers, write ways you could reach out to them in the lines below and the results as you acted on them.

_____

_____

_____

_____

Prayer Requests

Lesson 4

Condemnation of the Good Person

Romans 2:1-16

In college, I regularly went with a group of my friends to share the gospel. Over time, I realized I did not have a good grasp of the gospel.

After not being able to explain an defend my beliefs about heaven and hell, I realized the importance of understanding the gospel. I knew the gospel told you how to get to heaven. Since I wanted to go to heaven, I wanted to be clear how to get there! So I began to study the Bible to gain a mastery over the topic. Over time, I realized that the gospel was not so much about heaven, as having a relationship with God. Being with God is heaven.

Paul's letter to the Romans takes us through the gospel. He begins by showing the common ways that people fail to have a relationship with God. Then he tells us how we can know him. I remember the three groups of unsaved people by slightly changing the title of an old western movie, The Bad, The Good, and The Ugly. The bad do not care about knowing God. The good try to please him by their moral lifestyle. The ugly claim to be his followers, but think their religion saves them. In reality, God saves us when we place our faith in Jesus. God requires no works. He gives us salvation as a free gift.

Review:

What is the gospel?

Part 1

Proof:

Part 2

Proof:

Why is this good news?

Review

Romans 2:1-2:4

2:1 Therefore you have no excuse, everyone of you who passes judgment, for in that which you judge another, you condemn yourself; for you who judge practice the same things. 2 And we know that the judgment of God rightly falls upon those who practice such things. 3 But do you suppose this, O man, when you pass judgment on those who practice such things and do the same yourself, that you will escape the judgment of God? 4 Or do you think lightly of the riches of His kindness and tolerance and patience, not knowing that the kindness of God leads you to repentance?

Many people think they will go to heaven based on their good behavior.

Paul responds, "No. You are never good enough to have a relationship with God." You can never actually be righteous.

Judgment - The truth is that we all sin.

We should not make a judgement on other's relationship with God based on actions because we sin too.

When I attended Oklahoma State a man stood in the quad loudly condemning people to hell. I heard him condemn one girl because her skirt was too short. We called him Preacher Bob. He claimed that he no longer sinned and all people who sin go to hell.

People confronted him and asked him if he had

sped even one mile an hour. He said, "No." They asked if he had boasted about anything (which was obvious to us because he boasted about his righteousness.) They asked him if he had disobeyed his parents. He denied all of these sins. If he had done any of these things, he had condemned himself to separation from God by the basis of his deeds.

Then one time a student caught him in a sin. Preacher Bob then said, "It was not a sin, it was just a mistake." Preacher Bob did not understand that everyone sins. Everyone deserves death.

Romans 2:2 tells us that everyone who sins gets God's judgment. Romans 3:23 tells us that everyone sins. Sadly, we all sin and because of this sin, we receive the judgment of God. To be judged by God means we can not approach God for eternity. The Bible calls being separate form God, hell.

Three principles of judging?
#1 Matt. 18:15-17, Luke 17:3-4

Sit down one-on-one, and if they don't listen, you involve more people or the church.

#2 Romans 14:1-12

Don't judge them on something not in Scripture.

#3 Romans 2:1-4

You can't judge purely off of actions because you don't know someone's heart.

Romans 2:5-8

5 But because of your stubbornness and unrepentant heart you are storing up wrath for yourself in the day of wrath and revelation of the righteous judgment of God, 6 who will render to each person according to his deeds: 7 to those who by perseverance in doing good seek for glory and honor and immortality, eternal life; 8 but to those who are selfishly ambitious and do not obey the truth, but obey unrighteousness, wrath and indignation.

How does God judge who goes to heaven and who does not?

Revelation 20:11-15

Then I saw a great white throne and Him who sat upon it, from whose presence earth and heaven fled away, and no place was found for them. 12 And I saw the dead, the great and the small, standing before the throne, and books were opened; and another book was opened, which is the book of life; and the dead were judged from the things which were written in the books, <u>according to their deeds</u>. 13 And the sea gave up the dead which were in it, and death and Hades gave up the dead which were in them; and they were judged, every one of them <u>according to their deeds</u>. 14 Then death and Hades were thrown into the lake of fire. This is the second death, the lake of fire. 15 And if anyone's name was not found written in the book of life, he was thrown into the lake of fire. [Underlining mine]

Your entrance to heaven is based on your deeds. If you are perfect you get in. If you ever sinned, you do not.

What are the two ways to get eternal life?

1. (2:7) *Be perfect*

Who was the only person in human history to be saved in this way? *Jesus*

2. (1:16) (3:23) & (6:23) *Believing in Jesus*

Since we sin, we must receive eternal life from Jesus.

Romans 2:9-11

⁹ There will be tribulation and distress for every soul of man who does evil, of the Jew first and also of the Greek, ¹⁰ but glory and honor and peace to everyone who does good, to the Jew first and also to the Greek. ¹¹ For there is no partiality with God.

The consequences of sin and perfection

1. **The person who does evil gets**
   tribulation and distress

2. **The person who does good gets**
   glory, honor, and peace

What if you took a class where the professor told you that you had to get a 100% to pass the class. Then the professor had questions on the test well beyond your skill level. It would be impossible for you to get a 100%.

Knowing this, he gives the class two options. You could study your hardest and hope for the best or allow him to take the test, and receive whatever grade he scored on the test.

In a sense God offers us the same choice. God knew we could not be perfect, so he sent Jesus who lived the perfect life. If we trust Jesus, God gives us Jesus' righteousness. We avoid condemnation for our sin.

Romans 2:12-16

[12] For all who have sinned without the Law will also perish without the Law, and all who have sinned under the Law will be judged by the Law; [13] for it is not the hearers of the Law who are just before God, but the doers of the Law will be justified. [14] For when Gentiles who do not have the Law do instinctively the things of the Law, these, not having the Law, are a law to themselves, [15] in that they show the work of the Law written in their hearts, their conscience bearing witness and their thoughts alternately accusing or else defending them, [16] on the day when, according to my gospel, God will judge the secrets of men through Christ Jesus.

How does God judge the gentile who never had the law?

According to their conscience

God's Judgement of Jewish People

How do Jews and gentiles compare?

Gentiles: (vs. 12)

Perish without the law

Jews: (vs. 12)

Judged by the law

Jews: (vs. 13)

Not enough to only know the law

Gentiles: (vs. 15)

The law is written on our hearts

God condemns both Jews and gentiles unless they trust in Jesus Christ as savior.

What are the two things that tell us right from wrong?

1. *The Bible*
2. *Conscience*

Summary

Even good people deserve condemnation. Only Jesus lived perfectly. Even our best deeds appear dirty compared to God's holiness.

Discussion

How has it gone in reaching out to your friends who fit in the "bad" category?

Have you ever heard people say that you have to do good works to go to heaven? How should you respond to them?

How should we respond to someone who has sinned against us?

Do you struggle with being judgmental? How should we view our own righteousness?

Spiritual Development

Memorize Isaiah 64:6B

Read
Read Romans Chapter 2 three times this week on three different days. For accountability, write the date, time and location where you read it each of those three times.

#1

#2

#3

Pray
Write the names of at least 1 person you know that fits this category and pray for him/her every day this week.

As a result of your prayers, write ways you could reach out to them in the lines below and the results as you acted on them.

_____

_____

_____

_____

Prayer Requests

Lesson 5

Condemnation of the
Religious (Ugly) Person
Romans 2:17-29

Many people think their religious actions save them. They believe God requires them to be baptized, take communion, or confess theirs sins, for them to go to heaven. Romans corrects these wrong beliefs. We must be careful to not fall into the trap of thinking God requires our religious actions to save us. We also need to understand the gospel well enough to help people who have been misled.

In chapter 1 of Romans, we saw the bad person condemned because of their sin. Next we saw that the good person could not be good enough to earn his salvation. This lesson will show us that our religious activities do not contribute to our salvation.

Review

Paul systematically explains the different ways

people try to have a relationship with God and how all other than faith in Jesus apart from works lead to condemnation.

The first week we looked at the good news of Jesus Christ.

What is the gospel?

Proof:

Proof:

Why is this good news?

We cannot be with God because of our sin. Jesus Christ died for our sins as our substitute. He paid for our sins by dying on the cross and brings all who believe into fellowship with God. This means, if you believe in Jesus Christ, you can have a personal relationship with God and be confident you will spend eternity with Him.

Chapter 1 – The Bad person.

This person rejected the God of the Bible. God's responds, "OK. You will ruin your own life. I will let you do it." Their evil actions condemn them. They know better but do it anyway.

Chapter 2: The First Half - The Good Person

God condemns the good person because she falls short of perfection. God's holiness requires for people to be perfect to have a relationship with God and go to heaven. No one meets this standard because no one lives perfectly.

Today
Today we will study the second half of Chapter 2. The Religious (Ugly) person.

In this lesson, Paul will address if a person can please God through their religious activities. Can confession, baptism, repentance, going to church, or anything other religious activity save you?

Read 2:17-20
17 But if you bear the name "Jew" and rely upon the Law and boast in God, 18 and know His will and approve the things that are essential, being instructed out of the Law, 19 and are confident that you yourself are a guide to the blind, a light to those who are in darkness, 20 a corrector of the foolish, a teacher of the immature, having in the Law the embodiment of knowledge and of the truth,

What about Jews? Are they saved differently than gentiles? Paul begins with the positives of being a Jew, then shows they stand condemned with everyone else.

Benefit of being a Jew. (2:18-20)

1. (17)

2. (17)

3. (17)

4. (18)

5. (18)

6. (19)

7. (19)

8. (20)

9. (20)

Today, what religious actions do people rely on to get them to heaven?

No matter how many religious activities you do, you still fall into sin.

Romans 2:21-22

[21] you, therefore, who teach another, do you not teach yourself? You who preach that one shall not steal, do you steal? [22] You who say that one should not commit adultery, do you commit adultery? You who abhor idols, do you rob temples?

How did the Jews not practice what they preach?

1. (21)

2. (22)

3. (22)

Romans 2:23-24

[23] You who boast in the Law, through your breaking the Law, do you dishonor God? [24] For "the name of God is blasphemed among the Gentiles because of you," just as it is written.

What are the negative consequences of their sin?

1.

2.

We need to recognize that we struggle with similar sins to the ones we denounce.

Matt. 5:21-48

Romans 2:25-27

[25] For indeed circumcision is of value if you practice the Law; but if you are a transgressor of the Law, your circumcision has become uncircumcision. [26] So if the uncircumcised man keeps the requirements of the Law, will not his uncircumcision be regarded as circumcision? [27] And he who is physically uncircumcised, if he keeps the Law, will he not judge you who though having the letter of the Law and circumcision are a transgressor of the Law

What is the importance of circumcision?

What does Paul want the circumcised Jews to realize?

Jeremiah 4:4
Just as ritual circumcision cuts away the foreskin as an external symbol of dedicated covenant commitment, you must genuinely dedicate yourselves to the Lord and get rid of everything that hinders your commitment to me. (NET)

Romans 2:28-29

For he is not a Jew who is one outwardly, nor is circumcision that which is outward in the flesh. [29] But he is a Jew who is one inwardly; and circumcision is that which is of the heart, by the Spirit, not by the letter; and his praise is not from men, but from God.

What is God's desire for His followers?

Tommy, my best friend in college, served in church his entire life. Even when he went home on breaks, he helped the pastor on Sunday morning and took an active role in the church. Tommy thought he would get to heaven by his religious actions. In college he realized that these good religious activities could not save him because he still sinned. He trusted in Jesus Christ as savior and chose to be baptized as a believer.

Summary

Religious works cannot save you. No matter how many religious activities you do, you still sin and therefore stand condemned.

Discussion

Have you ever encountered a hypocritical Christian? Explain?

In what ways do you struggle with hypocrisy?

How can we call out sin as wrong, if we face similar struggles?

Spiritual Development

Memorize Romans 2:21

Read
Read Romans Chapter 3, three times this week on three different days. For accountability, write the date, time and location where you read it each of those three times.

#1

#2

#3

Pray
Write the names of at least 1 person you know that fits this category and pray for him/her every day this week.

As a result of your prayers, write ways you could reach out to them in the lines below and the results as you acted on them.

Prayer Requests

Lesson 6

Condemnation of All People

Romans 3:1-20

What do you live for?

A TV commercial boasted how you could watch every game happening in the country so you "don't miss those moments you live for!" It struck me the tragic nature of this commercial. How many people live for sports, travel, music, success, relationships or anything else other than God?

To people who live for sports, they talk about them all week, can't wait until the weekend to sit and watch. Their friends and family know to not plan anything on Monday nights or the weekend because of the games.

The first of the ten commandments state, "You shall have no other gods before me." We commit idolatry when we live for something other than God. This does not mean that we cannot enjoy sports or other entertainment, but if you look to the game to give you a sense of peace or help you find fulfillment in life, then you committed idolatry.

When people return from short term mission trips in third world countries, people comment, "They had nothing but had such joy." This comment bothered me because this implies they believe you need the comforts of technology to bring you happiness and joy. It surprises them to find uncomfortable people who worship God filled with joy.

All people violate the first commandment. We all live for things other than God. Some students at the college I serve think they would be less fulfilled or they might be less of a person if they did not study the liberal arts. They do not realize for millennia before many of these Great books were even written, before Western Civilization existed, people lived wonderful lives of significance filled with love, joy, and peace. Though the liberal arts can be helpful if studied as an act of worship to God, it too can become an idol and lead people from God.

In Romans 3, Paul teaches us the reality of our sin. We all sin. We all do wrong. However, at the end of the chapter, he will tell us about the amazing salvation from our sin Jesus provides.

\

Review

Chapter 1: _Condemnation of the Bad_

Chapter 2 (1st half): _Condemnation of the Good_

Chapter 2 (2nd half): _Condemnation of the Ugly (Religious)_

Memory Verse

Romans 2:21

you then who teach others, do you not teach yourself?
While you preach against stealing, do you steal?

In this section Paul answers a series of questions that Jewish people would ask based on his teaching in chapters one and two.

In chapter two, Paul showed that being a Jew did nothing for you if your heart did not change. This begs the question:

Question #1: Why be a Jew if it does not save you?

Romans 3:1
Then what advantage has the Jew? Or what is the benefit of circumcision?

Paul answers the question in the next verse.

Romans 3:2
Great in every respect. First of all, that they were entrusted with the oracles of God.

How does Paul answer the question?

What are the oracles of God?

Scripture

Paul then asks another question.

Question #2: If some Jews are not saved, how is God faithful?

Romans 3:3
What then? If some did not believe, their unbelief will not nullify the faithfulness of God, will it?

Romans 3:4
May it never be! Rather, let God be found true, though every man be found a liar, as it is written, "That You may be justified in Your words, And prevail when You are judged."

How does Paul answer the question?

Question #3: How is God righteous if he punishes us for making Him look good?

Romans 3:5
But if our unrighteousness demonstrates the righteousness of God, what shall we say? The God who inflicts wrath is not unrighteous, is He? (I am speaking in human terms.)

"We can sin because it demonstrates God's grace!" "Sin makes God look good!" Noo...

Romans 3:6
May it never be! For otherwise, how will God judge the world?

How does Paul answer the question?

Question #4: If our sin makes God look good, then why not sin to do good for God?

Romans 3:7-8
But if through my lie the truth of God abounded to His glory, why am I also still being judged as a sinner? And why not say (as we are slanderously reported and as some claim that we say), "Let us do evil that good may come"? Their condemnation is just.

Romans 3:8b
Their condemnation is just.

How does Paul answer the question?

Question #5: Are we better than the people who think that their sin pleases God?

Romans 3:9a
What then? Are we better than they?

Romans 3:9b
Not at all; for we have already charged that both Jews and Greeks are all under sin;

How does Paul answer the question?

After answering the typical questions regarding condemnation from sin, Paul shows us the Biblical basis of that theology.

The New Testament has the same gospel as the Old Testament. The apostles taught us the message of the Old Testament and any time they were asked they had to back up the gospel, they turned to the Old Testament. Paul, like the other apostles, shows how the Old Testament teaches the gospel.

Morality of Mankind

Romans 3:10-12

[10] *as it is written, "THERE IS NONE RIGHTEOUS, NOT EVEN ONE;*

[11] *THERE IS NONE WHO UNDERSTANDS,*

THERE IS NONE WHO SEEKS FOR GOD;

[12] *ALL HAVE TURNED ASIDE, TOGETHER THEY HAVE BECOME USELESS;*

THERE IS NONE WHO DOES GOOD,

THERE IS NOT EVEN ONE."

No human:

(10) is righteous

(11) understands / seeks God

(11b)

(12b) does good

All humans: (12)

Description of body:

Romans 3:13-18

13 "THEIR THROAT IS AN OPEN GRAVE,

WITH THEIR TONGUES THEY KEEP DECEIVING,"

"THE POISON OF ASPS IS UNDER THEIR LIPS";

14 "WHOSE MOUTH IS FULL OF CURSING AND BITTERNESS";

15 "THEIR FEET ARE SWIFT TO SHED BLOOD,

16 DESTRUCTION AND MISERY ARE IN THEIR PATHS,

17 AND THE PATH OF PEACE THEY HAVE NOT KNOWN."

18 "THERE IS NO FEAR OF GOD BEFORE THEIR EYES."

What body parts does Paul describe quoting the Hebrew Scriptures?

1. *Mouth*   *Action: what you say*

2. *Feet*   *Action: What you do*

3. *Eyes*   *Action: What you see*

Summary

Romans 3:19-20

Now we know that whatever the Law says, it speaks to those who are under the Law, so that every mouth may be closed and all the world may become accountable to God; because by the works of the Law no flesh will be justified in His sight; for through the Law comes the knowledge of sin.

What is the purpose of the Law?

Discussion

Does the Bible view people as inherently good or inherently bad?

How does the fallen condition of man affect how we live as Christians?

Some people who go to church say that we may not be able to be saved by the works of the Law, but we must be baptized, take communion, or going to confirmation to be saved? After studying Romans 1-3, how would you respond?

Others say we cannot be saved BY our works but we get grace THROUGH our works? Based on Romans 1-3, how would you respond?

Through FAITH

Spiritual Development

Memorize Romans 3:10

Read

Read Romans Chapter 3, three times this week on three different days. For accountability, write the date, time and location where you read it each of those three times.

#1

#2

#3

Pray

Write the names of at least 1 person you know who does not know Christ.

As a result of your prayers, write ways you could reach out to them in the lines below and the results as you acted on them.

_____

_____

_____

_____

Prayer Requests

Prayer Requests

Lesson 7

Justification Through Faith

Romans 3:21-31

Soon after I moved to Hillsdale, I asked some Christian leaders at Hillsdale College a simple question, "What percentage of the student body is Christian?" One leader said, "99%". Another said, "Not that many, maybe 2/3." Another said, "No, 20%." Then a few people said, "Maybe 50/50."

Conservatives can mistakenly label moral and religious people as Christians. They make this mistake because conservatives hold to Christian principles and Christian ideals.

Imagine a moral Hillsdale student who prays, goes to church and sings songs of worship. Is this person a Christian? What about a professor who is humble, loving, educated, and wise? What about a student passionate about their church and the teachings of their pastors. Who understands their beliefs and can defend them?

In Romans 3:21-31, Paul teaches what makes a

person a Christian. No matter, how wonderful you are, no matter how devoutly you go to church, no matter how much you pray and serve Jesus, you cannot save yourself. We must believe in Jesus accepting the free gift of salvation, or when we see Jesus, He will say, "Depart from me I never knew you."

Review

Chapter 1 _____

Chapter 2 (1st half) _____

Chapter 2 (2nd half) _____

Chapter 3 (1st half) _____

Memory Verse Review

Romans 3:10
[10] *as it is written, "THERE IS NONE RIGHTEOUS, NOT EVEN ONE;*

We have spent the last few weeks understanding how God pours out his wrath on all men because all men sin.

So how can we be saved from this impending doom?

Romans 3:21-22
But now apart from the Law the righteousness of God has been manifested, being witnessed by the Law and the Prophets, even the righteousness of God through faith in Jesus Christ for all those who believe; for there is no distinction

What does Paul mean by, "The righteousness of God has been manifested?"

Paul makes it clear that following God's commands cannot save us. So what is the purpose of the Old Testament?

Romans 3:23
For all have sinned and fall short of the glory of God

All have sinned

Fall short of the glory of God

Romans 3:24
being justified as a gift by His grace through the redemption which is in Christ Jesus;

Justified

Gift

Grace

Redemption

Romans 3:25

whom God displayed publicly as a propitiation in His blood through faith. This was to demonstrate His righteousness, because in the forbearance of God He passed over the sins previously committed;

Propitiation/atonement

Forbearance

Romans 3:26

for the demonstration, I say, of His righteousness at the present time, so that He would be just and the justifier of the one who has faith in Jesus.

What does Paul mean when he says, "He will be just and justifier?"

Romans 3:27

Where then is boasting? It is excluded. By what kind of law? Of works? No, but by a law of faith.

Why can we not boast?

You can not boast about receiving a free gift.

Romans 3:28

For we maintain that a man is justified by faith apart from works of the Law.

Justified

Nothing that we do will cause God to declare us righteous. To become righteous, we must accept Jesus' righteousness as a free gift.

Romans 3:29-30

Or is God the God of Jews only? Is He not the God of Gentiles also? Yes, of Gentiles also, since indeed God who will justify the circumcised by faith and the uncircumcised through faith is one.

Romans 3:31

Do we then nullify the Law through faith? May it never be! On the contrary, we establish the Law.

If we are saved apart from works, is the Law nullified?

Discussion

Have you encountered people confused about how to be saved?

How have you been confused about how to be saved?

How should you respond to someone who claims to be Christian but says you must do works in order to be saved?

How should we respond to someone who thinks you can actually become righteous instead of having Jesus righteousness given to you?

Spiritual Development

Memorize Romans 3:23-24

Read

Read Romans Chapter 4, three times this week on three different days. For accountability, write the date, time and location where you read it each of those three times.

#1

#2

#3

Share

Prepare the story of how you came to place your faith in Jesus Christ.

Share your testimony with someone once this week with someone, whether they are a known believer or not. For accountability write who and when you shared below.

_____

Pray

Pray for opportunities to share your faith with someone this week.

Prayer Requests

Lesson 8:

Is Justification by Faith Something New?

Romans 4

Review

Chapter 1   _____

Chapter 2 (1st half) _____

Chapter 2 (2nd half) _____

Chapter 3 (1st half) _____

Chapter 3 2nd half _____

A few years ago, I befriended and shared the gospel with a few Mormon missionaries. They claimed that the Bible had become distorted sometime between the time of Jesus and the fourth century AD. They believe Joseph Smith corrected the distortions the early church brought into the Bible.

We studied Romans chapter four to demonstrate the error of their thinking. The Old Testament teaches the same gospel as the New Testament. The dead sea scrolls of the Old Testament date back to 250 years before Jesus and teach the same gospel we have today. The dead sea scrolls prove the message of the Old Testament did not change.

They had no response to these facts. Finally after a long pause one responded, "I had a warm feeling when I read the book of Mormon so I know it is true."

When someone claims a truth about God, we must confirm it with scripture. Recently, someone asked me about praying to people instead of praying to God. I encouraged them to give all their devotion to God instead of splitting it between God and deceased people.

They responded that praying to dead people glorifies God since they simply request prayer from them. At this point, my mind went blank, and I asked for some time to think and pray about it. I should have said, "Show me in the Bible where it tells us to pray to people? Show me in the Bible where Jesus, or any of the apostles prayed to people? Where in the Old Testament did they pray to people?"

Even if we can not explain the flaw, if we make someone show us the truth taught in scripture, it protects us from our own lack of understanding. Of course it is wrong to pray to people. Never in the Bible does God smile upon or command us to pray to a dead person. We are to give all of our devotion to God. 1 Timothy 2:5 "For there is one God, and there is one mediator between God and men, the man Christ Jesus."

In Acts 17:11 The Berean people checked Paul's gospel against the scripture, "Now these were more noble-minded than those in Thessalonica, for they received the word with great eagerness, examining the Scriptures daily to see whether these things were so." If the Bible complemented the Bereans for making the Apostle Paul show them his teaching in the Bible, we should too!

We should not look to scripture to validate our ideas, but to start with Scripture and get our ideas from there. One time a guy tried to convince me the Bible taught purgatory. I asked him to show me and told him he could use the apocrypha too? He showed some verses that alluded to a place of the dead and smiled like he had showed me. I retorted you did not show me one passage that teaches this doctrine. Where does the Bible say we go to work off our sins after we die? Where does it teach this explicitly?

He could not show that because that gospel contradicts the gospel that Jesus saves us by grace alone. Our works have nothing to do with our salvation, Jesus gave us His righteousness as a free gift.

Some Christians think the Old Testament does not carry the authority of the New Testament. They must forget God wrote both the Old Testament and the New Testament. Though the New Covenant places us under grace instead of law, God saved people in the Old Testament and New Testament the same way. God is the same God.

In Romans four, Paul demonstrates the gospel he preaches comes from the Old Testament. He teaches justification by faith alone from the Old Testament. Since the first sin, God always saved people by faith alone.

God Saved Abraham by Faith Alone

Romans 4:1
What then shall we say that Abraham, our forefather according to the flesh, has found?

Why did Paul use Abraham as the example?

Romans 4:2

For if Abraham was justified by works, he has something to boast about, but not before God.

Justified

Boast

Why could Abraham not boast in his salvation?

Romans 4:3

For what does the Scripture say? "Abraham believed God, and it was credited to him as righteousness."

Believed

Credited

When Abraham believed God, God gave Abraham his righteousness as a free gift.

Romans 4:4

Now to the one who works, his wage is not credited as a favor, but as what is due.

Work

Favor

Due

What is Paul's point in verse four?

Romans 4:5

But to the one who does not work, but believes in Him who justifies the ungodly, his faith is credited as righteousness,

Did God save Abraham by faith, by works, or by a combination of faith and works?

What if Abraham had never performed a good work, would he be saved?

Work = due

No Work = Grace

According to Paul, can you say you are saved by grace and then claim you must work to be saved?

Is it possible to get grace through works?

God Saved David by Faith Alone

Genesis 15:6
"Abraham
believed
God and it
was credited
to him as
righteous-
ness."

Romans 4:6-8

*Just as David also speaks of the blessing on the man
to whom God credits righteousness apart from works:
"Blessed are those whose lawless deeds have been
forgiven, And whose sins have been covered. "Blessed is the
man whose sin the Lord will not take into account."*

**Did David teach that God saves by faith alone or
by faith and works?**

Can Anyone be Saved by Faith Alone?

Romans 4:9-12

*Is this blessing then on the circumcised, or on the
uncircumcised also? For we say, "FAITH WAS CREDITED TO
ABRAHAM AS RIGHTEOUSNESS."How then was it credited?
While he was circumcised, or uncircumcised? Not while
circumcised, but while uncircumcised; and he received the
sign of circumcision, a seal of the righteousness of the faith
which he had while uncircumcised, so that he might be the
father of all who believe without being circumcised, that
righteousness might be credited to them, and the father of
circumcision to those who not only are of the circumcision,
but who also follow in the steps of the faith of our father
Abraham which he had while uncircumcised.*

Can anyone be saved by grace?

Genesis 15:6

Genesis 17:23

Romans 4:13-16
 For the promise to Abraham or to his descendants that he would be heir of the world was not through the Law, but through the righteousness of faith. For if those who are of the Law are heirs, faith is made void and the promise is nullified; for the Law brings about wrath, but where there is no law, there also is no violation.

Were the promises to Abraham based on the Law or based on faith?

What were the promises to Abraham?

Why would faith have been made void if it was based on the Law?

What does Paul mean, "Where there is no law, there is no violation?"

Psalm 32:1-2

Romans 4:16-22

For this reason it is by faith, in order that it may be in accordance with grace, so that the promise will be guaranteed to all the descendants, not only to those who are of the Law, but also to those who are of the faith of Abraham, who is the father of us all, (as it is written, "A FATHER OF MANY NATIONS HAVE I MADE YOU") in the presence of Him whom he believed, even God, who gives life to the dead and calls into being that which does not exist. In hope against hope he believed, so that he might become a father of many nations according to that which had been spoken, "SO SHALL YOUR DESCENDANTS BE." Without becoming weak in faith he contemplated his own body, now as good as dead since he was about a hundred years old, and the deadness of Sarah's womb; yet, with respect to the promise of God, he did not waver in unbelief but grew strong in faith, giving glory to God, and being fully assured that what God had promised, He was able also to perform. Therefore IT WAS ALSO CREDITED TO HIM AS RIGHTEOUSNESS.

What does Paul mean, "It is by faith, in order that it may be in accordance with grace"?

What did Abraham believe?

Romans 4:23-25

Now not for his sake only was it written that it was credited to him, but for our sake also, to whom it will be credited, as those who believe in Him who raised Jesus our Lord from the dead, He who was delivered over because of our transgressions, and was raised because of our justification.

How was it for our sake that it was written that Abraham was credited with righteousness?

Discussion

How do you struggle believing in God's promises?

God shows us so much grace. How can we show grace to others?

Since our salvation has nothing to do with our works, how does this affect our confidence in going to heaven?

Spiritual Development

Memorize Romans 4:4-5

Read

Read Romans Chapter 5, three times this week on three different days. For accountability, write the date, time and location where you read it each of those three times.

#1

#2

#3

Forgive

If there is someone whom you are angry or who is angry with you, pray for them and work to reconcile by showing grace this week.

Share

Share your testimony with someone once this week with someone, whether they are a known believer or not. For accountability write who and when you shared below.

_____

Pray

Pray for opportunities to share your faith with someone this week.

Prayer Requests

Lesson 9

Rejoice!
Romans Chapter 5:1-11

The Bible tells us to do five things all the time. Meditate on the Word, pray, rejoice, be ready to share the gospel, and abound in good works.

I knew Bible study, prayer, serving and sharing the gospel drove my walk with God, but rejoicing? When I think God's attributes and actions, I rejoice. When I stop rejoicing, I have lost sight of Jesus and what I have as his child. I forget the temporary nature of my trials and that I will emerge victorious.

When I do not rejoice, I forget that God can use negative circumstances for my good. When I remember to take full advantage of the trial to learn, rejoicing comes naturally as I anticipate growth of character and faith.

When I do not rejoice, I forget my close relationship with God and the blessing that brings.

The five "always" commands work together. As we stay focused on God through Bible study, and prayer, then rejoicing, sharing our faith, and serving come much easier.

In Romans 5, Paul rejoices for the implications of the gospel and then ponders how Jesus fixed the problems with humanity that Adam broke.

Review

Chapter 1 _____

People who know right form wrong, but did wrong anyway.

Chapter 2 (1st half) _____

People who try to do good, but still sin so they stand condemned.

Chapter 2 (2nd half) _____

People who think they can please God through religious activities. They still sin so they stand condemned.

Chapter 3 (1st half) _____

All people sin and stand condemned.

Chapter 3 (2nd half)_____

    Only faith in Jesus Christ can save us from our sin The gift of salvation comes separate from works.

Chapter 4   _____

    People have always been saved by grace through faith. God saved Abraham through faith.

Part 1: Benefits of Believing

Let's examine some benefits of believing.

Romans 5:1
Therefore, having been justified by faith, we have peace with God through our Lord Jesus Christ,

What is a benefit of justification (5:1)?

Romans 5:2
Through him we have also obtained access by faith into this grace in which we stand, and we rejoice in hope of the glory of God. (ESV)

According to verse 2, what did we obtain from Christ?

Access

We rejoice because we have peace with God. In the next section, Paul tells us three ways we should rejoice. As justified people, we have privileged access to God. For the rest of eternity, we enjoy learning about and experiencing God because of His grace.

3 Areas of Rejoicing.

1. *(5:2) Hope of the Glory of God*
2. *(5:3) Tribulations*
3. *(5:11) We rejoice in God because Jesus Reconciled us to Him*

Romans 5:2b
we rejoice in hope of the glory of God. (ESV)

#1 WE REJOICE IN THE HOPE OF THE GLORY OF GOD

The word rejoice has the same root as Romans 2:17, 23, 3:27, and 4:2.

Glory of God

The hope of the glory of God has shone upon us through the gospel, which testifies that we shall be participators of the Divine nature; for when we shall see God face to face, we shall be like him. (2 Peter 1:4; 1 John 3:2.) - John Calvin Commentary on Romans 5:2

Romans 5:3-5

3 Not only that, but we rejoice in our sufferings, knowing that suffering produces endurance, 4 and endurance produces character, and character produces hope, 5 and hope does not put us to shame, because God's love has been poured into our hearts through the Holy Spirit who has been given to us. (ESV)

#2 WE REJOICE IN OUR TRIBULATIONS

Why would we rejoice when things go wrong?

->   ->   ->

Perseverance

Proven Character

Hope

Shame

Love

#3 WE REJOICE IN GOD BECAUSE JESUS RECONCILED US TO HIM (11)

Romans 5:6-8

For while we were still helpless, at the right time Christ died for the ungodly. For one will hardly die for a righteous man; though perhaps for the good man someone would dare even to die. But God demonstrates His own love toward us, in that while we were yet sinners, Christ died for us.

Why is it so amazing that Jesus Christ would die for us? (5:7-8)

Romans 5:9-11

Much more then, having now been justified by His blood, we shall be saved from the wrath of God through Him. For if while we were enemies we were reconciled to God through the death of His Son, much more, having been reconciled, we shall be saved by His life. And not only this, but we also exult in God through our Lord Jesus Christ, through whom we have now received the reconciliation.

What four ways does of Jesus death and resurrection impact our lives?

#1

#2

#3

#4

Summary

Jesus took us from being enemies of God to being friends of God.

Notice the structure of the passage.

#1 We rejoice in hope of the Glory of God the Father. (Future)

#2 We rejoice in our tribulations because of the work of the Holy Spirit in our lives. (Present)

#3 We rejoice that Jesus Christ changed us from being enemies to friends of God. (Past.)

Paul outlines how we rejoice in the work of the trinity.

How should this lesson help you to rejoice in the Lord?

Discussion

What importance have you placed on rejoicing in your Christian life?

What reasons did Paul give that would help us rejoice in God more?

What hard situations have you encountered that has made it difficult for you to rejoice?

Spiritual Development

Memorize Romans 5:3
Read

Read Romans Chapter 5, three times this week on three different days. For accountability, write the date, time and location where you read it each of those three times.

#1

#2

#3

Rejoice

Watch you attitude this week. Work to rejoice in all things. Each evening note the difference that has made in your life.

Thursday -

Friday -

Saturday -

Sunday -

Monday -

Tuesday -

Wednesday -

Pray

Pray for opportunities to share your faith with someone this week.

Prayer Requests

imputed:
to charge
to one's
account

Lesson 10

Jesus Fixed What Adam Broke
Romans 5:12-21

We use many bottles of super glue in our house. The kids favorite toys get broken and they come to me to fix it. When I went to Africa, I brought Joey, my two year old son, a hand carved wooden Zebra. Within two minutes he broke a leg. I glued it and gave it back to him the next day. A couple minutes later, he broke the leg in a different spot. More glue. Recently he climbed on the shelf to reach Asher's giraffe. More glue.

When we look around the world, we observe brokenness. Broken relationships, broken families, broken lives, broken governments. Even tornados, earthquakes, forest fires, and other natural disasters demonstrated the brokenness of the world.

Is there any glue that can fix the brokenness?

Today we will examine who broke the world and who fixes it.

Review

Chapter 1 _____

People who know right form wrong, but did wrong anyway.

Chapter 2 (1st half) _____

People who try to do good, but still sin so they stand condemned.

Chapter 2 (2nd half) _____

People who think they can please God through religious activities. They still sin so they stand condemned.

Chapter 3 (1st half) _____

All people sin and stand condemned.

Chapter 3 (2nd half)_____

Only faith in Jesus Christ can save us from our sin The gift of salvation comes separate from works.

Chapter 4 _____

People have always been saved by grace through faith. God saved Abraham through faith.

Chapter 5 _____

Rejoice because God has blessed us.

Romans 5:12

Therefore, just as through one man sin entered into the world, and death through sin, and so death spread to all men, because all sinned—

How did sin enter the world?

What was the result of the spread of sin?

Romans 5:13

for until the Law sin was in the world, but sin is not imputed when there is no law.

Why was sin not charged to a person's account when there was no law (5:13)?

Romans 5:14

Nevertheless death reigned from Adam until Moses, even over those who had not sinned in the likeness of the offense of Adam, who is a type of Him who was to come.

Why did death reign from Adam until Moses, even though sin was not charged against their accounts?

Theologians call this Original Sin.

We see Adam was a type of Jesus. What is a type?

Romans 5:15-19
But the free gift is not like the transgression. For if by the
transgression of the one the many died, much more did
the grace of God and the gift by the grace of the one Man,
Jesus Christ, abound to the many. The gift is not like that
which came through the one who sinned; for on the one
hand the judgment arose from one transgression resulting
in condemnation, but on the other hand the free gift arose
from many transgressions resulting in justification. For if
by the transgression of the one, death reigned through the
one, much more those who receive the abundance of grace
and of the gift of righteousness will reign in life through
the One, Jesus Christ. So then as through one transgression
there resulted condemnation to all men, even so through
one act of righteousness there resulted justification of life
to all men. For as through the one man's disobedience the
many were made sinners, even so through the obedience
of the One the many will be made righteous.

COMPARISON OF ADAM AND JESUS

Adam	Jesus
1. (15)	1. (15)
2. (16)	2. (16)
3. (17)	3. (17)
4. (18)	4. (18)
5. (19)	5. (19)

Romans 5:20-21

The Law came in so that the transgression would increase; but where sin increased, grace abounded all the more, so that, as sin reigned in death, even so grace would reign through righteousness to eternal life through Jesus Christ our Lord.

The Law existed for what purpose?

Discussion

Are people good or bad? Why?

How many times is the word gift used in Romans 5:15-19? What is this gift and why does it matter?

How does knowing you are in Christ instead of in Adam change your day to day life?

Spiritual Development

Memorize Romans 5:12

Read

Read Romans Chapter 5, three times this week on three different days. For accountability, write the date, time and location where you read it each of those three times.

#1

#2

#3

Reflect

As a human we either follow Adam or Jesus. Reflect on the difference between how these two leaders operate. See also Galatians 5:16-26 where the flesh is following Adam and the Spirit is following Jesus.

How does Christian morality grow from this understanding of right and wrong? In light of this understanding, can you explain why Jesus would make the claims of Matthew 5:21-48?

Pray

Pray for an opportunity to tell someone following Adam about the free gift Jesus offers.

Prayer Requests

Lesson 11

Why not sin?
Romans Chapter 6

When people understand that God loves us and saves us totally apart from our actions, sometimes people react saying, "*If what I do does not keep me from heaven, why can't I do anything I want?" Other people respond, "I know I am living in sin, but it is okay because God loves me anyway."

People tend to make two types of errors regarding the gospel. They want to keep works as part of the gospel. They will say, "I know you are saved by grace but you must work too." Theologians call this false gospel legalism. Others go to the opposite extreme. They think you can sin and God does not mind. They become antinomians.

In Chapter 4, Paul explained how legalists do not understand the gospel. TIn chapter 6, he addresses antinomians.

Review

Chapter 1 _____

People who know right form wrong, but did wrong anyway.

Chapter 2 (1st half) _____

People who try to do good, but still sin so they stand condemned.

Chapter 2 (2nd half) _____

People who think they can please God through religious activities. They still sin so they stand condemned.

Chapter 3 (1st half) _____

All people sin and stand condemned.

Chapter 3 (2nd half) _____

Only faith in Jesus Christ can save us from our sin The gift of salvation comes separate from works.

Chapter 4 _____

People have always been saved by grace through faith. God saved Abraham through faith.

Chapter 5 (1st Half) _____

    Rejoice because God has blessed us.

Chapter 5 (2nd Half)_____

    What Adam broke Jesus fixed.

Romans 5:20-6:1
The Law came in so that the transgression would increase; but where sin increased, grace abounded all the more, so that, as sin reigned in death, even so grace would reign through righteousness to eternal life through Jesus Christ our Lord.

What does Paul mean by where sin increased, grace abounded all the more?

Romans 6:1
What shall we say then? Are we to continue in sin so that grace may increase?

Two reasons we do not sin as Christians

1. We died. Sin no longer has any power over us.
Romans 6:2-14

2. We are no longer under the power of sin.
Romans 6:15-23

We do not Sin Because We Died

Romans 6:2

May it never be! How shall we who died to sin still live in it?

Romans 6:3-5

Or do you not know that all of us who have been baptized into Christ Jesus have been baptized into His death? Therefore we have been buried with Him through baptism into death, so that as Christ was raised from the dead through the glory of the Father, so we too might walk in newness of life. For if we have become united with Him in the likeness of His death, certainly we shall also be in the likeness of His resurrection,

What does Paul mean "baptized into His death?"

What does Paul mean by as Christ was raised from the dead, we might walk in newness of life?

Does this passage teach or imply we must be baptized to be saved?

Why is Baptism important if it does not save you?

Based on Romans 6:3-5, does immersion or sprinkling seem to communicate more clearly what has happened internally when we have trusted in Christ as our savior?

How does the principle of baptism teach us that we should not sin any longer (6:3-5)?

Romans 6:6-9

knowing this, that our old self was crucified with Him, in order that our body of sin might be done away with, so that we would no longer be slaves to sin; for he who has died is freed from sin. Now if we have died with Christ, we believe that we shall also live with Him, knowing that Christ, having been raised from the dead, is never to die again; death no longer is master over Him.

Why did we decide to follow Jesus?

How did we get rid of our body of sin?

Romans 6:10-11

For the death that He died, He died to sin once for all; but the life that He lives, He lives to God. Even so consider yourselves to be dead to sin, but alive to God in Christ Jesus.

How should we model our life after Jesus?

Romans 6:12-13

Therefore do not let sin reign in your mortal body so that you obey its lusts, and do not go on presenting the members of your body to sin as instruments of unrighteousness; but present yourselves to God as those alive from the dead, and your members as instruments of righteousness to God.

What should we do?

Romans 6:14

For sin shall not be master over you, for you are not under law but under grace.

Why should we not sin?

Summary

Two masters:

1. <u>Sin - Our desires</u>

2. <u>God - His desires</u>

Which master do you serve?

When you face temptation, remind yourself, "I do not have to do this sin because I am no longer under sin's authority."

Discussion

Do you consider yourself to be dead to sin? Why or why not?

How does this passage deepen your understanding of baptism?

Have you been baptized as a believer? Would you like to be baptized?

How should we respond to someone who says, "It is okay that I am sinning because we all sin. That's why we have God's grace right?"

Spiritual Development

Memorize Romans 6:10-11

Read

Read Romans Chapter 6, three times this week on three different days. For accountability, write the date, time and location where you read it each of those three times.

#1

#2

#3

Reflect

Reflect on what it means to die to your passions. How fully have you crucified the flesh with its desires?

How does viewing yourself as a slave of God change your perspective on life?

Confess

Confess areas where you have not died to sin.

Pray

Pray for opportunities to encourage others who are struggling.

Pray for opportunities to share the gospel this week.

Prayer Requests

Lesson 12

Why not sin?

Romans Chapter 6:15-23

We love freedom. As Americans we will fight and die for our freedom. Sometimes people mistakenly think, "It is okay that I sin because God will forgive me!" Most often this excuse comes as a result of sexual sin. They do not realize that they just abandoned the message of the gospel and moved to a heresy called Antinomianism.

According to Paul, every person either serves sin or God. We can choose to be slaves of sin and act in accordance to the desires of our body, or we can be slaves of God and act according to the desires of God. Being a slave to God frees us from sin.

God did not free us from the bondage of sin so that we would sin more. We must repent of our sin and live holy.

Each of us has a choice. Either we will follow our desires to sin or we will follow God's desires to righteousness. God leaves us no middle ground.

Review

Chapter 1 _____

    People who know right form wrong, but did wrong anyway.

Chapter 2 (1st half) _____

    People who try to do good, but still sin so they stand condemned.

Chapter 2 (2nd half) _____

    People who think they can please God through religious activities. They still sin so they stand condemned.

Chapter 3 (1st half) _____

    All people sin and stand condemned.

Chapter 3 (2nd half) _____

    Only faith in Jesus Christ can save us from our sin The gift of salvation comes separate from works.

Chapter 4 _____

    People have always been saved by grace through faith. God saved Abraham through faith.

Chapter 5 (1st Half) _____

    Rejoice because God has blessed us.

Chapter 5 (2nd Half)_____

    What Adam broke Jesus fixed.

Chapter 6   _____

    Why not sin?

After hearing about grace often people think they can serve God and sin. Paul condemns that view. He taught in the first half or Romans 6 that we do not sin because we died. Our death released us from the power of sin in our lives.

In this section, Paul gives us the second reason why we should not sin. If we understand the consequences of sin, why would we want to still sin? It doesn't make any sense to still sin!

Romans 6:15

What then? Shall we sin because we are not under law but under grace? May it never be!

Romans 6:16

Do you not know that when you present yourselves to someone as slaves for obedience, you are slaves of the one whom you obey, either of sin resulting in death, or of obedience resulting in righteousness?

What is the result of sin? (6:16,19)

What is the result of righteousness? (6:16,19)

Romans 6:17-18
But thanks be to God that though you were slaves of sin, you became obedient from the heart to that form of teaching to which you were committed, and having been freed from sin, you became slaves of righteousness.

Romans 6:19
I am speaking in human terms because of the weakness of your flesh. For just as you presented your members as slaves to impurity and to lawlessness, resulting in further lawlessness, so now present your members as slaves to righteousness, resulting in sanctification.

What does Paul mean by human terms?

What does Paul want them to do?

Romans 6:20-22

For when you were slaves of sin, you were free in regard to righteousness. Therefore what benefit were you then deriving from the things of which you are now ashamed? For the outcome of those things is death. But now having been freed from sin and enslaved to God, you derive your benefit, resulting in sanctification, and the outcome, eternal life.

What are the costs and benefits of the two masters we can choose?

Summary

Romans 6:23

For the wages of sin is death, but the free gift of God is eternal life in Christ Jesus our Lord.

Wage

Free Gift

Eternal life in Christ Jesus

Our Lord

Summary

Discussion

Why does Paul say we are slaves of something, either sin or God? Is it possible to be totally free?

How does it help us to ponder the consequences of our sin?

What sin do you struggle? What are the negative consequences of that sin in your life?

Spiritual Development

Memorize Romans 6:23

Read

Read Romans Chapter 7, three times this week on three different days. For accountability, write the date, time and location where you read it each of those three times.

#1

#2

#3

Reflect

Reflect on areas where you struggle with sin. Ponder the negative consequences of that sin in your life.

Confess

Talk with a mentor about those areas and seek counsel and accountability to chose God over that sin.

Pray

Repent of that sin and take the necessary steps to abandon that sin, choosing Jesus instead.

Pray for opportunities to share the gospel this week.

Lesson 13

The Law
Romans Chapter 7

How many of you have ever struggled with a sin? No matter how much you tried, you kept sinning the same way. You would get accountability, you would form a Christian community, you would think about how you would resist the sin, but in the end, you would sin again.

Do Christians have to settle for a pattern of failure that can not be broken? A life where we constantly go back to the same sin and approach God asking for forgiveness again and again? Is there any hope of real change?

Over the next couple lessons, Paul will share his experience with the Law and living in a continual pattern of sin and defeat. Then he will teach us how to walk by the Spirit and gain victory over sin in our life.

Review

Section 1: _____

Chapter 1: Bad

People who know right form wrong, but did wrong anyway.

Chapter 2 (1st half): Good

People who try to do good, but still sin so they stand still condemned.

Chapter 2 (2nd half): Ugly

People who think they can please God through religious activities. They still sin so they stand condemned.

Chapter 3 (1st half): All Sinned

All people sin and stand condemned.

Chapter 3 (2nd half): Christian

The only way to get salvation is by faith in Jesus Christ. Salvation is given as a gift apart from works.

Chapter 4: Abraham

Salvation by grace through faith is not new. Abraham was saved that way.

Chapter 5: Adam

Everything that Adam broke Jesus Fixed

Section 2: _____

Chapter 6: Why not sin?

Reason #1 _____

Reason #2 _____

In Romans 7 and 8 Paul will contrast the result of living by the Law and living by the Spirit.

Romans 7:1-3

Or do you not know, brethren (for I am speaking to those who know the law), that the law has jurisdiction over a person as long as he lives? For the married woman is bound by law to her husband while he is living; but if her husband dies, she is released from the law concerning the husband. So then, if while her husband is living she is joined to another man, she shall be called an adulteress; but if her husband dies, she is free from the law, so that she is not an adulteress though she is joined to another man.

How can a person not be under the jurisdiction of the Law anymore?

Romans 7:4

Therefore, my brethren, you also were made to die to the Law through the body of Christ, so that you might be joined to another, to Him who was raised from the dead, in order that we might bear fruit for God.

What is the purpose of becoming a Christian?

What does it mean to bear fruit for God?

Romans 7:5-6

For while we were in the flesh, the sinful passions, which were aroused by the Law, were at work in the members of our body to bear fruit for death. But now we have been released from the Law, having died to that by which we were bound, so that we serve in newness of the Spirit and not in oldness of the letter.

In the flesh

How did the law affect us?

What is the believer's relationship to the Law?

Romans 7:7a

What shall we say then? Is the Law sin? May it never be!

Romans 7:7b-12

On the contrary, I would not have come to know sin except through the Law; for I would not have known about coveting if the Law had not said, "You shall not covet." But sin, taking opportunity through the commandment, produced in me coveting of every kind; for apart from the Law sin is dead. I was once alive apart from the Law; but when the commandment came, sin became alive and I died; and this commandment, which was to result in life, proved to result in death for me; for sin, taking an opportunity through the commandment, deceived me and through it killed me. So then, the Law is holy, and the commandment is holy and righteous and good.

Is the Law sin?

What function does the law serve?

Romans 7:13

Therefore did that which is good become a cause of death for me? May it never be! Rather it was sin, in order that it might be shown to be sin by effecting my death through that which is good, so that through the commandment sin would become utterly sinful.

Did the Law cause us to die?

Romans 7:14-25

For we know that the Law is spiritual, but I am of flesh, sold into bondage to sin. For what I am doing, I do not understand; for I am not practicing what I would like to do, but I am doing the very thing I hate. But if I do the very thing I do not want to do, I agree with the Law, confessing that the Law is good. So now, no longer am I the one doing it, but sin which dwells in me.

For I know that nothing good dwells in me, that is, in my flesh; for the willing is present in me, but the doing of the good is not. For the good that I want, I do not do, but I practice the very evil that I do not want. But if I am doing the very thing I do not want, I am no longer the one doing it, but sin which dwells in me. I find then the principle that evil is present in me, the one who wants to do good. For I joyfully concur with the law of God in the inner man, but I see a different law in the members of my body, waging war against the law of my mind and making me a prisoner of the law of sin which is in my members. Wretched man that I am! Who will set me free from the body of this death? Thanks be to God through Jesus Christ our Lord! So then, on the one hand I myself with my mind am serving the law of God, but on the other, with my flesh the law of sin.

What does Paul mean when he says (7:14), "For we know that the Law is spiritual, but I am of flesh, sold into the bondage of sin."

What does Paul mean by, "The willing is present in me, but the doing of the good is not." (7:17)

What does Paul mean in verses 17 and 20, "I am no longer the one doing it, but sin which dwells in me?"

There is an internal war within you in regards to following the law or sin. How does it feel in your life when you face that war?

How do we try to defeat sin using the Law?

How can we be free of this struggle and defeat?

Discussion

Why does trying to follow a set of rules always fail?

Do you ever feel like verse 15, "I am not practicing what I would like to do but am doing the very thing I hate?"

How should we engage in the battle against sin, if fighting it by Law does not work?

Spiritual Development

Memorize Romans 7:4

Read

Read Romans Chapter 8, three times this week on three different days. For accountability, write the date, time and location where you read it each of those three times.

#1

#2

#3

Reflect

Reflect on how you combat sin. Do you work to follow a set of rules?

Confess

Talk with a mentor about fight sin and seek counsel about how to fight sin by the Spirit instead of by the law.

Pray

Repent of that sin and take the necessary steps to abandon that sin, choosing Jesus instead.

Pray for opportunities to share the gospel this week.

Lesson 14

Living By the Spirit
Romans Chapter 8:1-25

Christians know we need to walk by the Spirit. However, many Christians do not seem to understand exactly how to walk by the Spirit. Many fall into the trap of Romans 7 and continue walking by rules and experience the cycle of failure that comes from that approach.

In Romans Chapter 8, Paul teaches that walking by the Spirit means that we set our minds on the things of the Spirit. After we have died to ourselves, we must stop thinking about ourselves and what we want. We must think instead about the Lord and what he wants.

Shifting our thinking from ourselves to God, lifts our minds to the close relationship we have with God and the hope we have eternally.

Review

Section 1: _____

Chapter 1: Bad

These are people who know right form wrong, but did wrong anyway.

Chapter 2 (1st half): Good

These are people who try to do good, but still sin so they are still condemned.

Chapter 2 (2nd half): Ugly

These are people who think they can please God through religious activities. They still sin so they are condemned.

Chapter 3 (1st half): All Sinned

All people sin and all people are condemned.

Chapter 3 (2nd half): Christian

Only faith in Jesus Christ can save us from our sin The gift of salvation comes separate from works.

Chapter 4: Abraham

People have always been saved by grace through faith. God saved Abraham through faith.

Chapter 5: Adam

Everything that Adam broke Jesus Fixed

SECTION 2: _____

Chapter 6: Why not sin?

Reason #1 _____

Reason #2 _____

Chapter 7 _____

We cannot be holy by following a set of rules.

In Chapter 7, Paul explained the cycle of trying to be holy through rules. We try hard not to sin, then sin, then try even harder not to sin and sin again. Each time feeling more and more guilty and condemned.

Today we are going to examine how to avoid that cycle and instead have victory in the Christian life by living by the Spirit.

Romans 8:1
Therefore there is now no condemnation for those who are in Christ Jesus.

What is the first thing Paul wants us to realize?

Romans 8:2-4
For the law of the Spirit of life in Christ Jesus has set you free from the law of sin and of death. For what the Law could not do, weak as it was through the flesh, God did: sending His own Son in the likeness of sinful flesh and as an offering for sin, He condemned sin in the flesh, so that the requirement of the Law might be fulfilled in us, who do not walk according to the flesh but according to the Spirit.

What did Jesus do for us?

Romans 8:5-8
For those who are according to the flesh set their minds on the things of the flesh, but those who are according to the Spirit, the things of the Spirit. For the mind set on the flesh is death, but the mind set on the Spirit is life and peace, because the mind set on the flesh is hostile toward God; for it does not subject itself to the law of God, for it is not even able to do so, and those who are in the flesh cannot please God.

What must we do to live by the Spirit?

What does it mean to set our mind on things of the Spirit?

How do you set your mind on things of the Spirit?

Romans 8:9
However, you are not in the flesh but in the Spirit, if indeed the Spirit of God dwells in you. But if anyone does not have the Spirit of Christ, he does not belong to Him.

"In the Spirit" versus "In the flesh"

Does every Christian have the Holy Spirit?

Romans 8:10-11

If Christ is in you, though the body is dead because of sin, yet the spirit is alive because of righteousness. But if the Spirit of Him who raised Jesus from the dead dwells in you, He who raised Christ Jesus from the dead will also give life to your mortal bodies through His Spirit who dwells in you.

What is our present reality as Christians?

What will the Spirit do for us?

#1 Set your mind on what God wants.

Romans 8:12-13

So then, brethren, we are under obligation, not to the flesh, to live according to the flesh—for if you are living according to the flesh, you must die; but if by the Spirit you are putting to death the deeds of the body, you will live.

How are we to live as Christians?

If someone says she trusted in Christ but never lives any different, is she saved?

Romans 8:14-17

For all who are being led by the Spirit of God, these are sons of God. For you have not received a spirit of slavery leading to fear again, but you have received a spirit of adoption as sons by which we cry out, "Abba! Father!" The Spirit Himself testifies with our spirit that we are children of God, and if children, heirs also, heirs of God and fellow heirs with Christ, if indeed we suffer with Him so that we may also be glorified with Him.

How do we know if someone is a Christian?

What does the Spirit tell us about our relationship with God?

Matthew 6:6
But when you pray, go into your room and shut the door and pray to your Father who is in secret. And your Father who sees in secret will reward you.

Why does suffering play a major role in Paul's view of the Christian life?

#2 Setting our mind on our hope for the future helps us deal with suffering

Romans 8:18

For I consider that the sufferings of this present time are not worthy to be compared with the glory that is to be revealed to us.

So how do we deal with the suffering that we face as Christians?

Romans 8:19-21

For the anxious longing of the creation waits eagerly for the revealing of the sons of God. For the creation was subjected to futility, not willingly, but because of Him who subjected it, in hope that the creation itself also will be set free from its slavery to corruption into the freedom of the glory of the children of God.

When Adam sinned, not only man fell, but all of creation fell as well.

What is creation's hope?

Romans 8:22-23

For we know that the whole creation groans and suffers the pains of childbirth together until now. And not only this, but also we ourselves, having the first fruits of the Spirit, even we ourselves groan within ourselves, waiting eagerly for our adoption as sons, the redemption of our body.

Why is the present suffering compared to childbirth?

What are the first fruits of the Spirit?

We are waiting for what?

Romans 8:24-25

For in hope we have been saved, but hope that is seen is not hope; for who hopes for what he already sees? But if we hope for what we do not see, with perseverance we wait eagerly for it.

Can you hope for something that is already there?

Discussion

How should we ourselves after being a Christian? (8:1)

What must we do to walk by the Spirit? (8:5)

How should we set our minds on the Spirit?

Spiritual Development

Memorize Romans 8:5

Read

Read Romans Chapter 8, three times this week on three different days. For accountability, write the date, time and location where you read it each of those three times.

#1

#2

#3

Read

Read Psalm 119 this week.

Meditate

Meditate on the memory verse, Romans 8:5. How can you keep your mind focused on things of the Spirit and not things of the flesh? How can you use Bible Study and prayer to help?

Work to set your minds on

#1 – Our position as sons of God

#2 – Our hope of the redemption of our body (the 2nd coming of Christ)

What are you doing to change your thinking? Is that sufficient?

Get Help

Talk with a friend or mentor about encouraging you in the battle of your mind.

Pray

For God to open conversations with people who go to church but appear to be walking by the flesh.

Lesson 15

Living By the Spirit

Romans Chapter 8:26-39

I remember praying to accept Jesus as my savior again and again and again. Shortly after praying, I would find myself sinning again and felt the need to pray the salvation prayer again to be sure. At night I would lay in bed and think about how I could be good enough to earn the love of my earthly father and the love of my heavenly father.

No matter how hard I tried, I never seemed to measure up. Each accomplishment would be eclipsed by the next challenge. The nagging question, "Are you good enough?" Never left my mind.

When I understood that Jesus loved me unconditionally and that my salvation could never be lost because I did nothing to earn it, I felt as if I instantly lost 50 pounds. People started asking me why I never quit smiling. It became much easier to give of myself and going to church became a joy instead of a burden. Knowing God loved me unconditionally fueled my walk as I served Him out of deep gratitude.

Review

Section 1: _____

Chapter 1: Bad

These are people who know right form wrong, but did wrong anyway.

Chapter 2 (1st half): Good

These are people who try to do good, but still sin so they are still condemned.

Chapter 2 (2nd half): Ugly

These are people who think they can please God through religious activities. They still sin so they are condemned.

Chapter 3 (1st half): All Sinned

All people sin and all people are condemned.

Chapter 3 (2nd half): Christian

Only faith in Jesus Christ can save us from our sin The gift of salvation comes separate from works.

Chapter 4: Abraham

People have always been saved by grace through faith. God saved Abraham through faith.

Chapter 5: Adam

Everything that Adam broke Jesus Fixed

SECTION 2: _____

Chapter 6: Why not sin?

Reason #1 _____

Reason #2 _____

Chapter 7 _____

We cannot be holy by following a set of rules.

Chapter 8: _____

To live a Godly life we must walk by the Spirit.

Last week learned to set our minds on the things of Spirit and not our desires. We need to reflect on our position with God and to live in hope of his coming.

In this lesson, we will examine God's amazing love for us.

God Helps Us

Romans 8:26-27

In the same way the Spirit also helps our weakness; for we do not know how to pray as we should, but the Spirit Himself intercedes for us with groanings too deep for words; and He who searches the hearts knows what the mind of the Spirit is, because He intercedes for the saints according to the will of God.

How does the Spirit help us?

Hebrews 7:25

Romans 8:28-30

And we know that God causes all things to work together for good to those who love God, to those who are called according to His purpose. For those whom He foreknew, He also predestined to become conformed to the image of His Son, so that He would be the firstborn among many brethren; and these whom He predestined, He also called; and these whom He called, He also justified; and these whom He justified, He also glorified.

What does it mean that God causes all things to work together for good to those who love God?

What is predestination?

Does predestination mean there is no free will?

Being Sure of Our Salvation Helps Us Walk by the Spirit

Romans 8:31

What then shall we say to these things? If God is for us, who is against us?

If God is for you, who is against you?

Romans 8:32-33

He who did not spare His own Son, but delivered Him over for us all, how will He not also with Him freely give us all things? Who will bring a charge against God's elect? God is the one who justifies;

How do we know God will not condemn us?

What about Jesus? Jesus judges the living and the dead. Could Jesus be the one who would condemn us?

Romans 8:34

Who is the one who condemns? Christ Jesus is He who died, yes, rather who was raised, who is at the right hand of God, who also intercedes for us.

Why would Jesus not condemn us?

Romans 8:35

Who will separate us from the love of Christ? Will tribulation, or distress, or persecution, or famine, or nakedness, or peril, or sword?

Who or what can condemn us?

Romans 8:36-37

Just as it is written,"FOR YOUR SAKE WE ARE BEING PUT TO DEATH ALL DAY LONG; WE WERE CONSIDERED AS SHEEP TO BE SLAUGHTERED." But in all these things we overwhelmingly conquer through Him who loved us.

Can these hardships condemn us?

Romans 8:38

For I am convinced that neither death, nor life, nor angels, nor principalities, nor things present, nor things to come, nor powers, nor height, nor depth, nor any other created thing, will be able to separate us from the love of God, which is in Christ Jesus our Lord.

Who or what can condemn us?

We Can not be Condemned By...

Death nor Life

Angels nor Principalities

Things Present nor Things to Come

Powers

Height nor Depth

Any Other Created Thing

The only thing not created is God and he already showed the God will not condemn us. Nothing can separate you from the Love of Christ. It is the love of Christ that keeps you from being condemned.

What about ourselves? Can we cause our own condemnation once we have been saved?

We walk in the Spirit by being secure in our salvation.

Discussion

Based on what we learned in 8:26-27 and Hebrews 7:25, how should we respond to people who think they need to have their pastor, a deceased saint, or Mary to pray for them in order for God to hear and answer?

Why does Paul make assurance of salvation such a big deal with regards to walking by the Spirit?

How can you help someone who thinks they can lose their salvation?

Spiritual Development

Memorize Romans 8:38

Read

Read Romans Chapter 9, three times this week on three different days. For accountability, write the date, time and location where you read it each of those three times.

#1

#2

#3

Meditate

Meditate on what you have as a Christian. Ponder how much God loves you and what it means to be secure in his love knowing you will spend eternity with Him.

Pray

For God to open conversations with people who go to church but appear to be walking by the flesh.

Prayer Requests